SELECTIONS FROM

VH1 Music First

100 GREATEST LOVE SONGS

The list of *100 Greatest Love Songs* was compiled by the production and music programming teams at VH1. The songs were not picked for their chart position, but for their emotion—which songs moved people the most and which songs best expressed feelings of love. The trick was, we didn't just want ballads.

We found there were many great rock songs that were love songs at their core, such as Cheap Trick's "I Want You to Want Me" and Led Zeppelin's "Whole Lotta Love." Love songs were chosen from every genre, from disco to rock to pop to power ballads...and we still left room for the classics by Sinatra, Elvis and The Righteous Brothers.

We believe these are the love songs for VH1 fans and proved our little theory that at the heart of almost every great song is one inspiration—love. Be it heartbreak or heartfelt joy, be it rock, pop or disco, love is what keeps these songs together.

—Michelle Mahoney, Executive Producer

ISBN 0-634-05654-9

HAL•LEONARD®
CORPORATION

7777 W. BLUEMOUND RD. P.O. BOX 13819 MILWAUKEE, WI 53213

Visit Hal Leonard Online at
www.halleonard.com

VH1 100 GREATEST LOVE SONGS

Ranking

RANK	SONG	ARTIST	YEAR
1.	I Will Always Love You	Whitney Houston	1992
2.	My Heart Will Go On (Love Theme from 'Titanic')	Celine Dion	1998
3.	Maybe I'm Amazed	Paul McCartney	1970
4.	Love Me Tender	Elvis Presley	1956
5.	Open Arms	Journey	1982
6.	Unchained Melody	The Righteous Brothers	1965
7.	Always on My Mind	Willie Nelson	1982
8.	Endless Love	Diana Ross & Lionel Richie	1981
9.	I'll Be There	The Jackson 5	1970
10.	I Don't Want to Miss a Thing	Aerosmith	1998
11.	At Last	Etta James	1961
12.	How Deep Is Your Love	The Bee Gees	1977
13.	Nothing Compares 2 U†	Sinead O'Connor	1990
14.	Fly Me to the Moon (In Other Words)	Frank Sinatra	1964
15.	I Honestly Love You	Olivia Newton-John	1974
16.	She's Got a Way	Billy Joel	1982
17.	You Are So Beautiful	Joe Cocker	1975
18.	In Your Eyes†	Peter Gabriel	1986
19.	If You Leave Me Now	Chicago	1976
20.	I Got You Babe	Sonny & Cher	1965
21.	You Don't Bring Me Flowers	Neil Diamond & Barbra Streisand	1978
22.	You're the One That I Want	Olivia Newton-John and John Travolta	1978
23.	Unforgettable	Natalie Cole with Nat "King" Cole	1991
24.	Wonderful Tonight	Eric Clapton	1978
25.	Breathe	Faith Hill	2000
26.	Babe	Styx	1979
27.	You're in My Heart	Rod Stewart	1978
28.	Let's Get It On	Marvin Gaye	1973
29.	Your Song	Elton John	1971
30.	Because You Loved Me	Celine Dion	1996
31.	You Are the Sunshine of My Life	Stevie Wonder	1973
32.	Woman	John Lennon	1981
33.	(Everything I Do) I Do It for You	Bryan Adams	1991
34.	Keep On Loving You	REO Speedwagon	1981
35.	Superstar	Carpenters	1971
36.	You're the First, The Last, My Everything	Barry White	1975
37.	Don't Speak	No Doubt	1996
38.	Crazy for You	Madonna	1985
39.	I'll Be There for You	Bon Jovi	1989
40.	You're Still the One	Shania Twain	1998
41.	Beth	Kiss	1976
42.	I Would Die 4U†	Prince	1985
43.	More Than Words	Extreme	1991
44.	(I've Had) The Time of My Life	Bill Medley & Jennifer Warnes	1987

RANK	SONG	ARTIST	YEAR
45.	Un-break My Heart	*Toni Braxton*	1996
46.	Let's Stay Together	*Al Green*	1972
47.	I'd Do Anything for Love (But I Won't Do That)	*Meat Loaf*	1993
48.	By Your Side	*Sade*	2001
49.	I Can't Make You Love Me	*Bonnie Raitt*	1992
50.	Always	*Atlantic Starr*	1987
51.	That's the Way Love Goes	*Janet Jackson*	1993
52.	Love Bites	*Def Leppard*	1988
53.	Mandy	*Barry Manilow*	1975
54.	Fallin'	*Alicia Keys*	2001
55.	Faithfully	*Journey*	1983
56.	The First Time Ever I Saw Your Face	*Roberta Flack*	1972
57.	I Want to Know What Love Is	*Foreigner*	1985
58.	Best of My Love	*The Emotions*	1977
59.	I'll Stand by You	*The Pretenders*	1994
60.	Three Times a Lady	*Commodores*	1978
61.	Alone	*Heart*	1987
62.	To Be with You	*Mr. Big*	1992
63.	How Do I Live	*LeAnn Rimes*	1997
64.	I Melt with You	*Modern English*	1983
65.	Here and Now	*Luther Vandross*	1990
66.	Iris	*Goo Goo Dolls*	1998
67.	Eternal Flame	*Bangles*	1989
68.	More Than a Feeling	*Boston*	1976
69.	Never Tear Us Apart	*INXS*	1988
70.	I Think I Love You	*The Partridge Family*	1970
71.	Whole Lotta Love†	*Led Zeppelin*	1970
72.	Love Will Keep Us Together	*Captain & Tennille*	1975
73.	Save the Best for Last	*Vanessa Williams*	1992
74.	I Feel for You†	*Chaka Khan*	1984
75.	Baby, I Love Your Way	*Peter Frampton*	1976
76.	Love to Love You, Baby	*Donna Summer*	1976
77.	All Cried Out	*Lisa Lisa & Cult Jam*	1986
78.	Sweet Child o' Mine	*Guns N' Roses*	1988
79.	I'll Be	*Edwin McCain*	1998
80.	Islands in the Stream	*Kenny Rogers & Dolly Parton*	1983
81.	Total Eclipse of the Heart	*Bonnie Tyler*	1983
82.	All Out of Love	*Air Supply*	1980
83.	I'll Make Love to You	*Boyz II Men*	1994
84.	Time After Time	*Cyndi Lauper*	1984
85.	Careless Whisper	*Wham! featuring George Michael*	1985
86.	Secret Garden†	*Bruce Springsteen*	1995
87.	Is This Love	*Whitesnake*	1987
88.	Thank You	*Dido*	2001
89.	I Want You to Want Me	*Cheap Trick*	1979
90.	Back at One	*Brian McKnight*	1999
91.	Alison	*Elvis Costello*	1977
92.	This I Promise You	**NSYNC*	2000
93.	We Belong	*Pat Benatar*	1985
94.	Nobody Wants to Be Lonely	*Ricky Martin with Christina Aguilera*	2001
95.	It Must Have Been Love	*Roxette*	1990
96.	I Just Want to Be Your Everything	*Andy Gibb*	1977
97.	Think of Laura	*Christopher Cross*	1984
98.	I Need Love	*LL Cool J*	1987
99.	Hero	*Enrique Iglesias*	2001
100.	Every Rose Has Its Thorn	*Poison*	1988

†Omitted from this publication because of licensing restrictions.

Contents

ALISON

Words and Music by
ELVIS COSTELLO

ALL CRIED OUT

Words and Music by BRIAN GEORGE, CURTIS BEDEAU,
GERARD CHARLES, LUCIEN GEORGE,
PAUL GEORGE and HUGH CLARKE

Female: All a-lone on a Sun-day morn-ing, out-side I see the rain is fall-ing, whoa. was I such a fool, la-dy, oh yes.

Male: Nev-er want-ed to see things your way. I had to go a-stray. Oh, why

Original key: D-flat major. This edition has been transposed up one half-step to be more playable.

ALL OUT OF LOVE

Words and Music by GRAHAM RUSSELL
and CLIVE DAVIS

ALONE

Words and Music by BILLY STEINBERG
and TOM KELLY

Original key: Db major. This edition has been transposed up one half-step to be more playable.

And now it chills me to the bone. How do I get ____ you a - lone? ____

____ How do I get ____ you a - lone? ____

Guitar solo ad lib.

ALWAYS

Written by JONATHAN LEWIS,
DAVID LEWIS and WAYNE LEWIS

Male: Girl, you are __ to me __
Come with me, __ my sweet; __

all __ that a wom-an should be, and I ded-i-cate __ my life to you al - ways. __ A
let's go make a fam-i-ly. And they will bring __ us joy for al - ways. __ Oh,

Female:

ALWAYS ON MY MIND

Words and Music by WAYNE THOMPSON,
MARK JAMES and JOHNNY CHRISTOPHER

BABY, I LOVE YOUR WAY

Words and Music by
PETER FRAMPTON

Shad - ows grow__ so long be - fore my
Moon ap - pears__ to shine and light the
I can see__ the sun - set in your

eyes and they're mov - ing a - of some and
sky with the help
eyes, brown and grey__

cross the page.__ Sud - den - ly__ the day__ turns in - to night__
fire - fly.__ Won - der how__ they have__ the pow'r to shine.__
blue be - sides.__ Clouds are stalk - ing is - lands in the sun.__

But don't hes - i - tate,___ 'cause your

love_____ won't___ wait.___

AT LAST

Lyric by MACK GORDON
Music by HARRY WARREN

I _____ can call my own. I __ found a thrill _____ to press my

cheek to, _____ a thrill that I _____ have nev - er

known. __ Oh, ___ yeah, _ yeah. _____ You smiled, ___ you smiled,

oh, ___ and then _____ the spell was cast, ___

and here___ we are _____ in heav - en,

Freely

for ___ you are mine _____ at ___ last. _____

a tempo

Freely

BABE

Words and Music by
DENNIS DeYOUNG

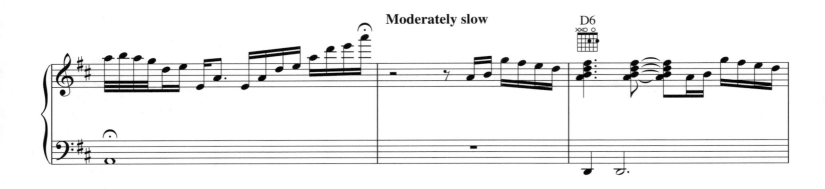

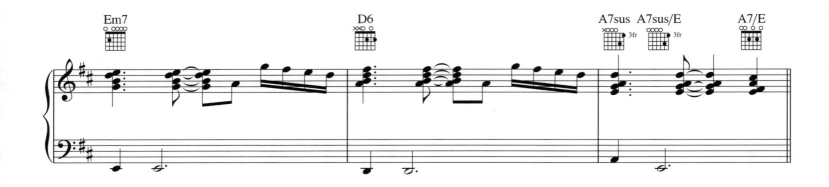

Babe, I'm leav-in'. I must be on___ my way.___ The time is draw-ing

BACK AT ONE

Words and Music by
BRIAN McKNIGHT

BECAUSE YOU LOVED ME

from UP CLOSE AND PERSONAL

Words and Music by
DIANE WARREN

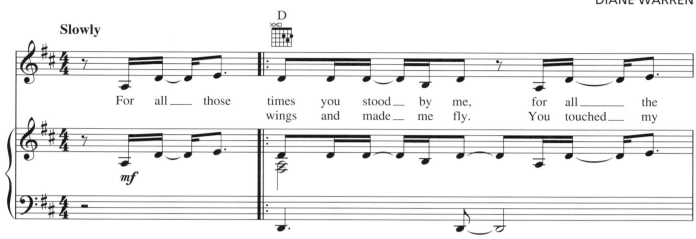

For all ___ those times you stood ___ by me, for all ___ the
wings and made ___ me fly. You touched ___ my

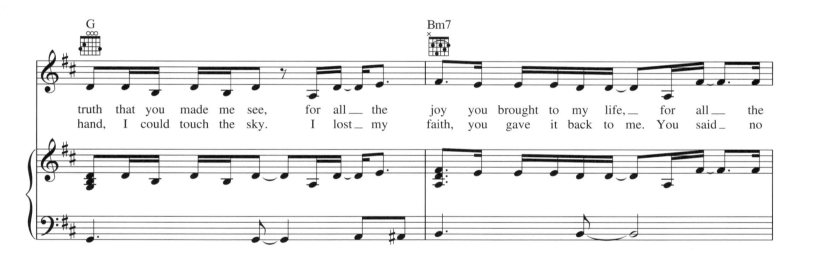

truth that you made me see, for all ___ the joy you brought to my life, ___ for all ___ the
hand, I could touch the sky. I lost ___ my faith, you gave it back to me. You said ___ no

wrong that you ___ made right, for ev - 'ry ___ dream you made ___ come true, for all ___ the
star was out ___ of reach. You stood ___ by ___ me and I ___ stood tall. I had ___ your

Original key: D♭ major. This edition has been transposed up one half-step to be more playable.

BEST OF MY LOVE

Words and Music by MAURICE WHITE
and AL McKAY

Does-n't take___ much to make___ me___ hap-py and make___ me smile____ with glee.___

Nev-er, nev-er will I feel____ dis-cour-aged 'cause our love's___ no mys-ter-y.____

CODA

Dem - on - strat - ing _____ sweet love and af - fec - tion

that you give _____ so _____ o - pen - ly, yeah. _____ The way I feel a - bout you

ba - by, can't ex - plain it, want the whole _____ wide _____ world _____ to see.

Repeat and Fade

Oh, oh, _____ oh, _____ oh, _____ oh, _____ oh, _____ you've got the best of my love.

BETH

Words and Music by PETER CRISS, BOB EZRIN
and STAN PENRIDGE

Rock Ballad, with feeling

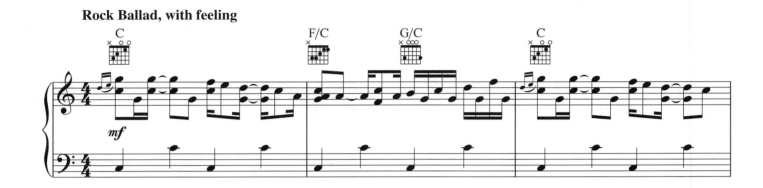

Beth, I hear you call - in', but I can't come home right now.
You say you feel so emp - ty, that our house just ain't a home.

Me and the boys are play - in' and we just can't find the sound.
I'm al - ways some - where else and you're al - ways there a - lone.

CARELESS WHISPER

Words and Music by GEORGE MICHAEL
and ANDREW RIDGELEY

BREATHE

Words and Music by HOLLY LAMAR
and STEPHANIE BENTLEY

Moderately fast

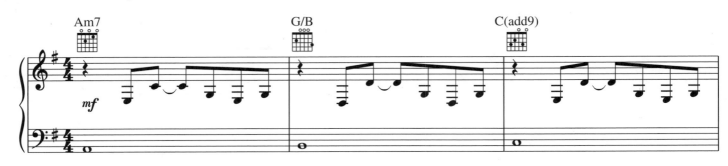

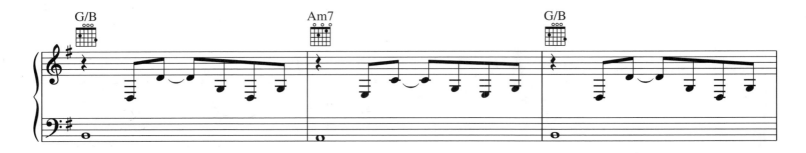

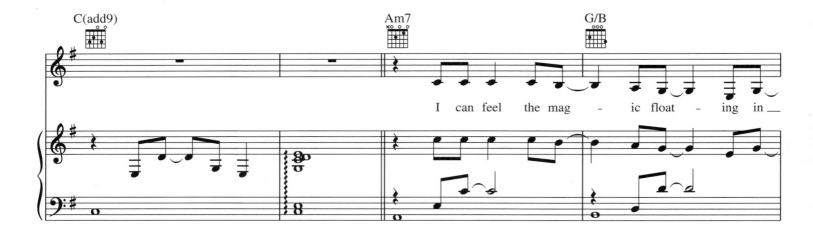

I can feel the mag - ic float - ing in

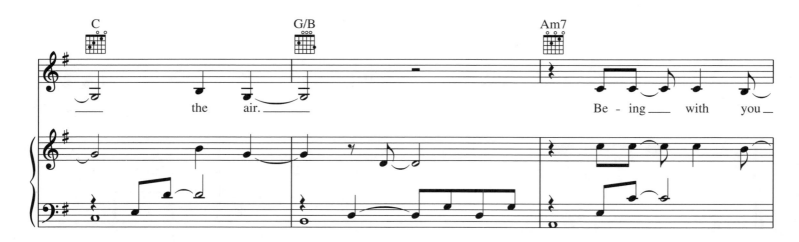

the air. ___ Be - ing ___ with you

BY YOUR SIDE

Words by SADE ADU
Music by SADE ADU,
STUART MATTHEWMAN, ANDREW HALE
and PAUL SPENCER DENMAN

Original key: B major. This edition has been transposed up one half-step to be more playable.

CRAZY FOR YOU
from VISION QUEST

Words and Music by JOHN BETTIS
and JON LIND

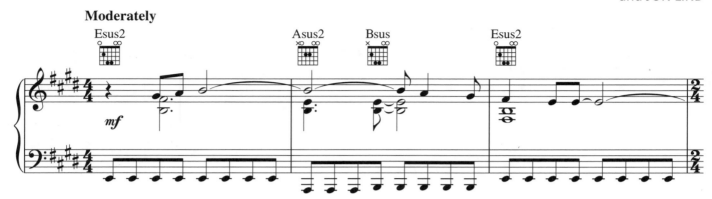

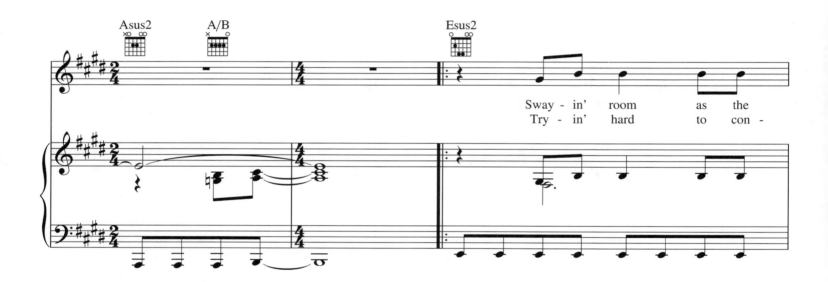

Sway-in' room as the
Try-in' hard to con-

mu-sic starts.___ Strang-ers mak-in' the most___ of the dark.___
trol my heart,___ I walk o-ver to where___ you___ are.___

DON'T SPEAK

Words and Music by ERIC STEFANI
and GWEN STEFANI

Lyrics (under staves):

You and me, we used to be to-geth-er, ev-'ry day to-geth-er, al-ways. I real-ly feel _____ that I'm los-ing my best _ friend. I can't be-lieve this could _ be the ___ end. It looks as though _ you're _

As we die, ___ both __

ENDLESS LOVE

from ENDLESS LOVE

Words and Music by
LIONEL RICHIE

Oh, _____ and _____ love, _____

cresc.

mf

ETERNAL FLAME

Words and Music by BILLY STEINBERG,
TOM KELLY and SUSANNA HOFFS

Original key: F♯ major. This edition has been transposed up one half-step to be more playable.

EVERY ROSE HAS ITS THORN

Words and Music by BRET MICHAELS, C.C. DeVILLE,
BOBBY DALL and RIKKI ROCKET

We both lie si-lent-ly still __ in the dead of the night. __ Al-though we

both lie close to-geth — er, __ we feel miles a-part __ in-side. __ Was it

some-thing I said or some-thing I did? Did my words not come out right? __ Though I

know that you'd be here right now if I could-'ve let you know some-how.__ I guess ev - 'ry rose has its

thorn, just like ev - 'ry night has its dawn. _____ Just like

ev - 'ry cow-boy __ sings his sad, sad __ song, ev - 'ry rose has its

thorn. Though it's been a - while __ now I can still feel so much pain.__

FAITHFULLY

Words and Music by
JONATHAN CAIN

FALLIN'

Words and Music by
ALICIA KEYS

Freely   N.C.

I keep on fall - in' in _____ *(Vocal ad lib.)* and

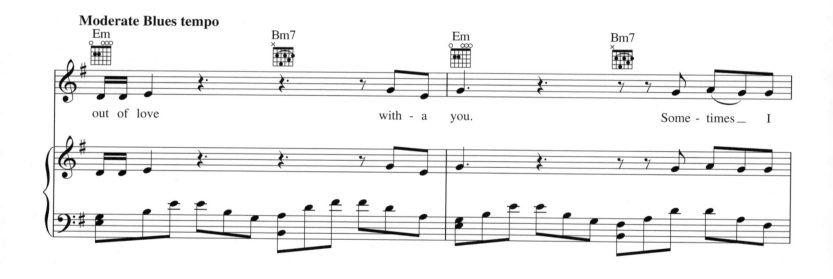

Moderate Blues tempo

out of love   with - a you.   Some - times__ I

love   you   some - times you make me blue.   Some-times I feel

love with a - you. I _____ nev - er loved some - one ____ the way that

I love a - you. What?

THE FIRST TIME EVER I SAW YOUR FACE

Words and Music by
EWAN MacCOLL

The first time ever I
The first time ever I
The first time ever I

saw your face,
kissed your mouth,
lay with you

I thought the sun
I felt the earth
and felt your heart

rose in your eyes,
move in my hand,
so close to mine,

FLY ME TO THE MOON
(In Other Words)
featured in the Motion Picture ONCE AROUND

Words and Music by
BART HOWARD

Bossa Nova

Fly me to the moon, and let me play a-mong the stars;

Let me see what spring is like on

Ju - pi - ter and Mars. In oth - er words,

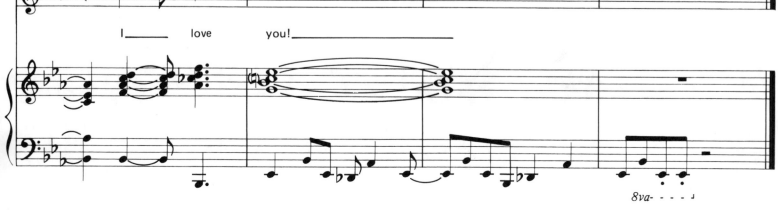

HERO

Words and Music by ENRIQUE IGLESIAS,
PAUL BARRY and MARK TAYLOR

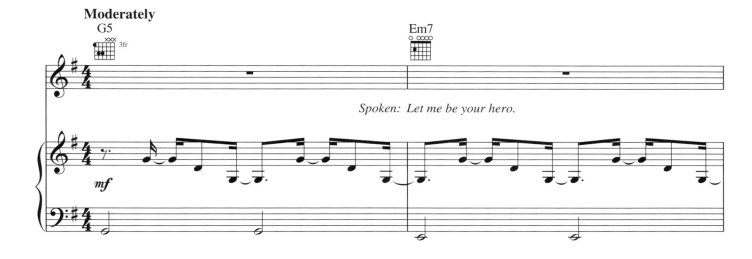

Spoken: Let me be your hero.

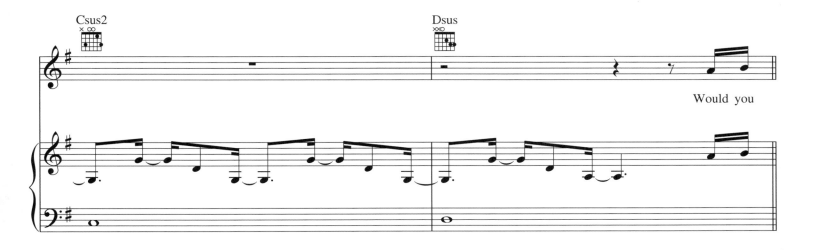

Would you

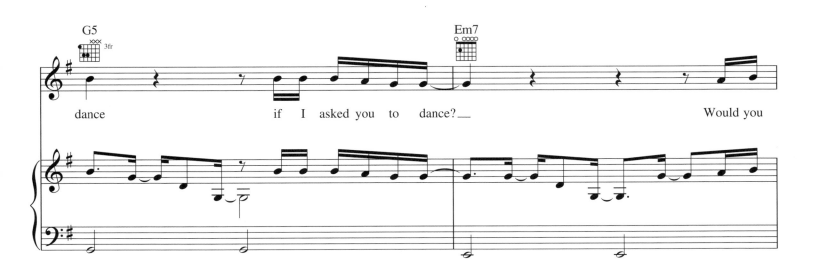

dance   if I asked you to dance?   Would you

HERE AND NOW

Words and Music by TERRY STEELE
and DAVID ELLIOT

HOW DEEP IS YOUR LOVE

from the Motion Picture SATURDAY NIGHT FEVER

Words and Music by BARRY GIBB,
MAURICE GIBB and ROBIN GIBB

I know your eyes in the morn-ing sun. ___ I feel you touch ___
I be-lieve in you. ___ You know the door ___

___ me in the pour-ing rain. ___ And the mo-ment that you wan-der far ___
___ to my ver-y soul. ___ You're the light ___ in my deep-est, dark-

___ from me, ___ I wan-na feel you in my arms a-gain. ___ And you come ___
-est hour; ___ you're my sav-ior when I fall. ___ And you may ___

(Everything I Do)
I DO IT FOR YOU

from the Motion Picture ROBIN HOOD: PRINCE OF THIEVES

Words and Music by BRYAN ADAMS,
ROBERT JOHN LANGE and MICHAEL KAMEN

Look in-to my eyes,_____
Look in-to your heart,_____

you will see____ what you mean to____ me.
you will find____ there's noth-ing there to____ hide.

Search your
Take me as I

heart,_____ search your soul,_____ and when you
am,_____ take my life,_____ I would

HOW DO I LIVE

Words and Music by
DIANE WARREN

Moderately slow

How do I ____ get through the night with-out ____ you? If I had to
there'd be no sun in my ____ sky. ____ There would be no

live with-out ____ you, ____ what kind of life would that be? _____ Oh, ____ I, ____
love in my ____ life. ____ There'd be no world left for me. _____ And ____ I, ____

I CAN'T MAKE YOU LOVE ME

Words and Music by MIKE REID
and ALLEN SHAMBLIN

I DON'T WANT TO MISS A THING

from the Touchstone Picture ARMAGEDDON

Words and Music by
DIANE WARREN

I GOT YOU BABE

Words and Music by
SONNY BONO

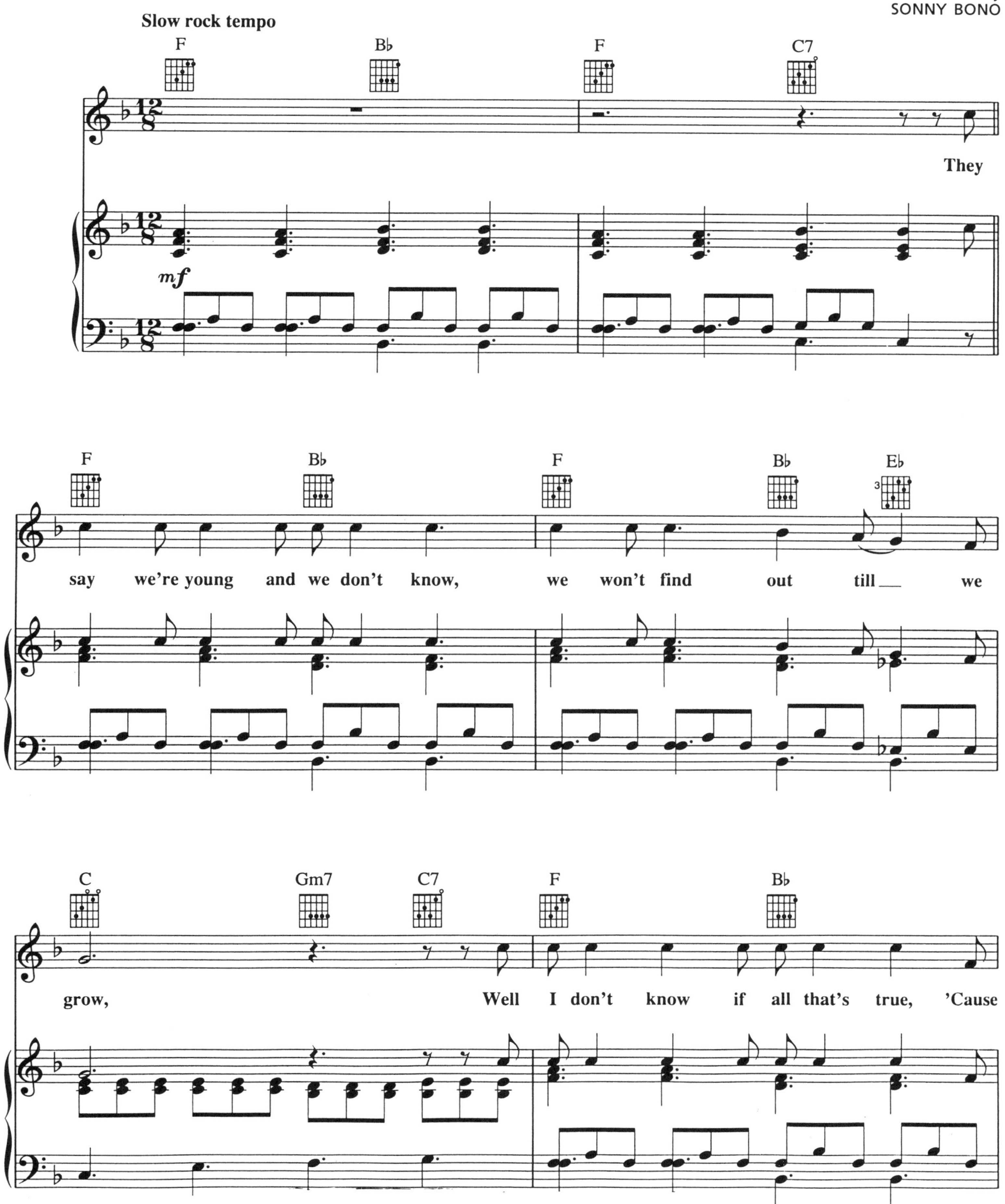

Slow rock tempo
F
B♭
F
C7
They
mf
F
B♭
F
B♭
E♭
say we're young and we don't know, we won't find out till — we
C
Gm7
C7
F
B♭
grow, Well I don't know if all that's true, 'Cause

Let them say your hair's too long, 'cause I don't care, with you I can't do wrong. _____ Then put your ____ lit-tle hand in mine, There ain't no hill or moun-tain we can't climb, babe, I got you, babe. I got

Repeat and Fade

I HONESTLY LOVE YOU

Words and Music by PETER ALLEN
and JEFF BARRY

I got some - thin' to tell___ you that I nev - er thought___ I would,
but
this is pure___ and sim - ple and you must re - a - lize that it's

I be - lieve___ you real - ly ought___ to know.___
com - in' from___ my heart and not___ my head.___

I love you, I hon - est - ly love___ you.

___ you.

I THINK I LOVE YOU
featured in the Television Series THE PARTRIDGE FAMILY

Words and Music by
TONY ROMEO

wor-ries me to say ___ that I'd nev - er felt ___ this way.

I JUST WANT TO BE YOUR EVERYTHING

Words and Music by
BARRY GIBB

Slowly, with a beat

For so long, _____ you and me been find-ing each oth-er

for so long. _____ And the feel-ing that I feel _____ for you is

more_____ than strong, girl. Take it from me. If you

Guitar Tacet

ev - 'ry - thing.

Dar - ling, for so

I MELT WITH YOU

Words and Music by RICHARD IAN BROWN,
MICHAEL FRANCIS CONROY, ROBERT JAMES GREY,
GARY FRANCES McDOWELL and STEPHEN JAMES WALKER

Mov - ing for -
Dream of bet -

- wards, us - ing all ___ my breath;
- ter lives, the kind ___ which nev - er hate. ___

To Coda ⊕

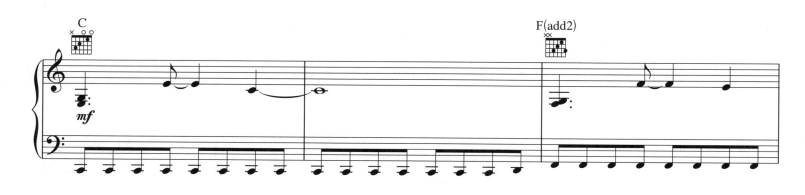

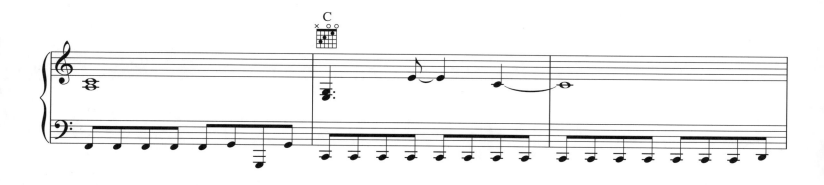

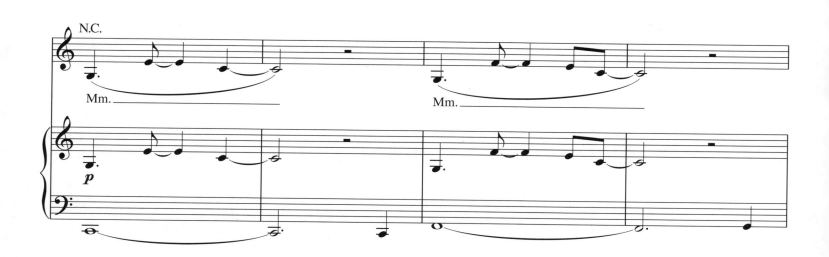

I NEED LOVE

Words and Music by JAMES TODD SMITH,
DWAYNE SIMON, BOBBY ERVING,
DARRYL PIERCE and STEVEN ETTINGER

Spoken: Girl, listen to me.

Rap Lyrics

1. There I was, giggling about the games
   That I had played with many hearts, and I'm not sayin' no more names.
   Then the thought occured, teardrops made my eyes burn
   As I said to myself, "Look what you've done to her."
   I can feel it inside; I can't explain how it feels,
   All I know is that I'll never dish another raw deal,
   Playin' make-believe, pretending that I'm true,
   Holding in my laugh as I say that I love you.
   Saying, "Amor," kissing you on the ear,
   Whispering, "I love you" and, "I'll always be here."
   Although I often reminisce, I can't believe that I found
   A desire for true love floatin' around
   Inside my soul. Because my soul is cold,
   One half of me deserves to be this way till I'm old.
   But the other half needs affection and joy,
   And the warmth that is created by a girl and a boy.
   I need love. I need love.

2. Romance, sheer delight, how sweet!
   I gotta find me a girl to make my life complete.
   You could scratch my back; we'll get cozy and huddle.
   I'll lay down my jacket so you can walk over a puddle.
   I'd give you a rose, pull out your chair before we eat,
   Kiss you on the cheek and say, "Ooh, girl, you're so sweet."
   It's deja vu whenever I'm with you;
   I could go on forever tellin' you what I'd do.
   But where you at? You're neither here nor there.
   I swear I can't find you anywhere.
   Damn sure ain't in my closet, or under my rug.
   This love search is really makin' me bug.
   And if you know who you are, why don't you make yourself seen?
   Take a chance with my love, and you'll find out what I mean.
   Fantasies can run, but they can't hide.
   And when I find you, I'm gonna pour all my love inside.
   I need love. I need love.

3. I wanna kiss you, hold you, never scold you, just love you,
   Suck on your neck, caress you and rub you,
   Grind, moan, and never be alone.
   If you're not standin' next to me, you're on the phone.
   Can't you hear it in my voice? I need love bad.
   I got money, but love's somethin' I've never had.
   I need your ruby red lips, sweet face and all.
   I love you more than a man who's ten feet tall.
   I watch the sun rise in your eyes.
   We're so in love, when we hug, we become paralyzed.
   Our bodies explode in ecstasy unreal.
   You're as soft as a pillow and I'm hard as steel.
   It's like a dreamland; I can't lie, I never been there.
   Maybe this is an experience that me and you can share.
   Clean and unsoiled, yet sweaty and wet.
   I swear to you, this is somethin' I'll never forget.
   I need love. I need love.

4. See what I mean? I've changed; I'm no longer
   A playboy on the run, I need somethin' that's stronger.
   Friendship, trust, honor, respect, admiration;
   This whole experience has been such a revelation.
   It's taught me love and how to be a real man,
   To always be considerate and do all I can,
   Protect you; you're my lady and you mean so much.
   My body tingles all over from the slightest touch
   Of your hand, and understand, I'll be frozen in time
   Till we meet face to face and you tell me your mind.
   If I find you, girl, I swear I'll be a good man;
   I'm not gonna leave it in destiny's hands.
   I can't sit and wait for my princess to arrive;
   I've gotta struggle and fight to keep my dream alive.
   I'll search the whole world for that special girl;
   When I finally find you, watch our love unfurl.
   I need love. I need love.

I WANT TO KNOW WHAT LOVE IS

Words and Music by
MICK JONES

change this lone - ly life._____ I want to know what love__ is.__

I want you to show__ me.

I want to feel what love_is.__ I know you can show__ me.__

D.S.% and fade

__ me.

I WANT YOU TO WANT ME

Words and Music by
RICK NIELSEN

Bright Two-Beat

(music staves with lyrics:)

want   you   to want ___ me.   I

need   you   to need ___ me.   I'd

love you to love ___ me. I'm

beg - gin' you to { beg me. / beg me. I'll } I

want you to want ___ me. I

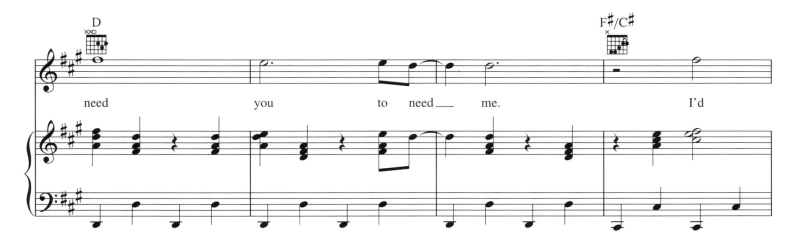

need you to need ___ me. I'd

I WILL ALWAYS LOVE YOU

Words and Music by
DOLLY PARTON

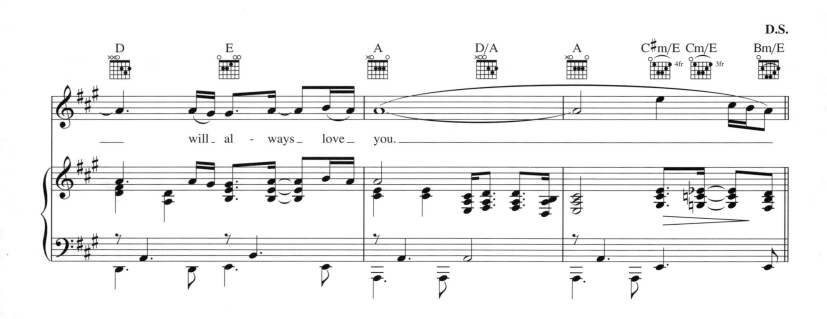

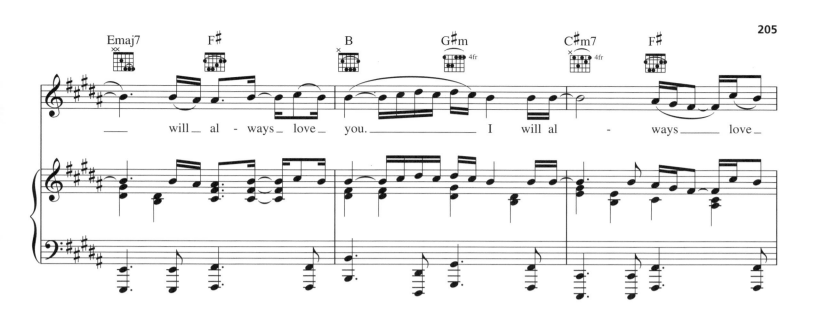

will al - ways love you. I will al - ways love

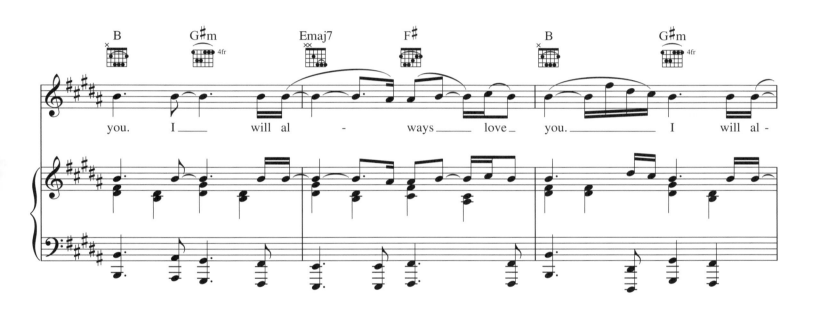

you. I will al - ways love you. I will al -

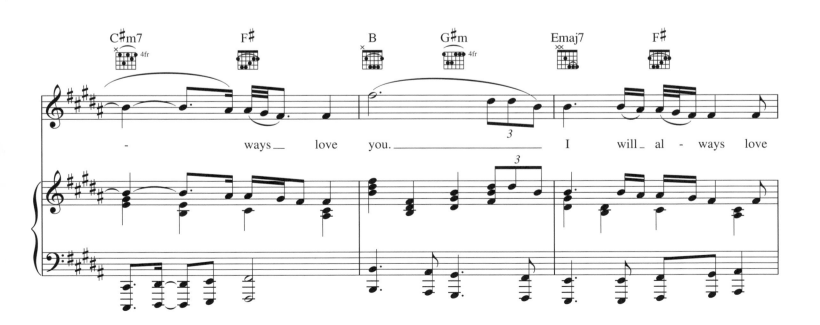

- ways love you. I will al - ways love

Additional Lyrics

3. I hope life treats you kind.
   And I hope you have all you've dreamed of.
   And I wish to you, joy and happiness.
   But above all this, I wish you love.

I'D DO ANYTHING FOR LOVE
(But I Won't Do That)

Words and Music by
JIM STEINMAN

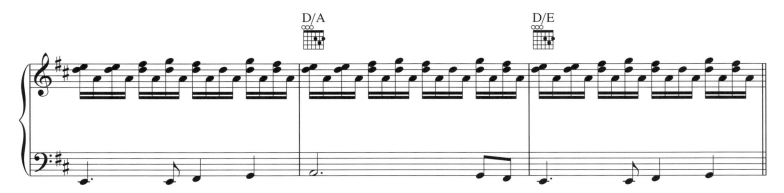

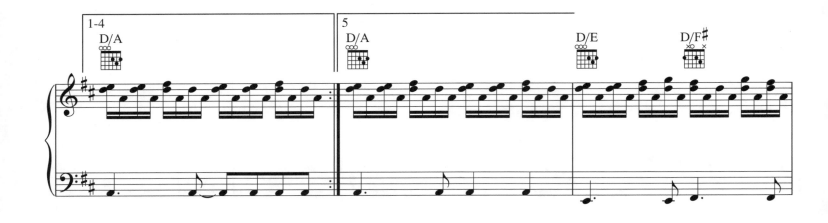

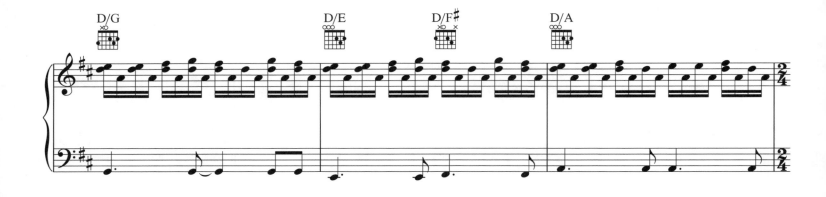

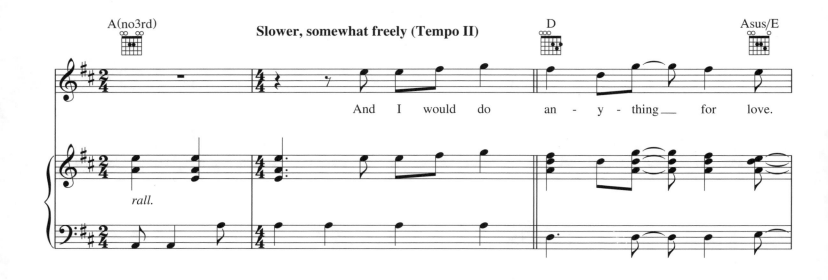

Slower, somewhat freely (Tempo II)

And I would do an-y-thing___ for love.

rall.

I'LL BE

Words and Music by
EDWIN McCAIN

Original key: B Major. This edition has been transposed up one half-step to be more playable.

I'LL BE THERE

Words and Music by BERRY GORDY,
HAL DAVIS, WILLIE HUTCH and BOB WEST

Just call my name _____ and I'll ___ be there. ___

Just call my name _____

and I'll ___ be there. _____

I'LL MAKE LOVE TO YOU

Words and Music by
BABYFACE

Slowly, in a steady 2

Close your eyes, make a wish, and blow
lax, let's go slow. I ain't

I'LL BE THERE FOR YOU

Words and Music by JON BON JOVI
and RICHIE SAMBORA

I'LL STAND BY YOU

Words and Music by CHRISSIE HYNDE,
TOM KELLY and BILLY STEINBERG

Moderately slow

Oh, why you look so sad, the tears are in your eyes, come on and come to me now. And don't be a-shamed to cry, let me see you through, 'cause I've seen the dark side too.

IF YOU LEAVE ME NOW

Words and Music by
PETER CETERA

Moderately slow
C G/C C G/C C G/C C G/C C G/C C
mf
Cmaj7 Am7
If you leave me now, you'll take a-way the big-gest part
leave me now, you'll take a-way the ver-y heart
Em7 Am7 D7
of me. Ooh, no, ba-by, please
of me. Ooh, no, ba-by, please
G 1 C G C 2 C
don't go. And if you
don't go. Ooh,

-row comes, ___ then we'll both ___ re - gret ___ the things we said ___ to - day. ___

IRIS
from the Motion Picture CITY OF ANGELS

Words and Music by
JOHN RZEZNIK

1
G
Gmaj7
2
Gmaj7
G
Bm
Bm7
2fr
Bm
G
Gmaj7
Bm
Bm9
Bm
G
Gmaj7
Bm (add4)
Bm11
Bm (add4)

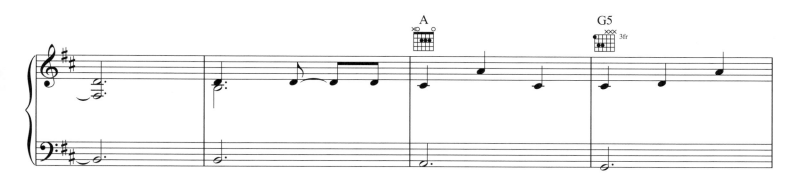

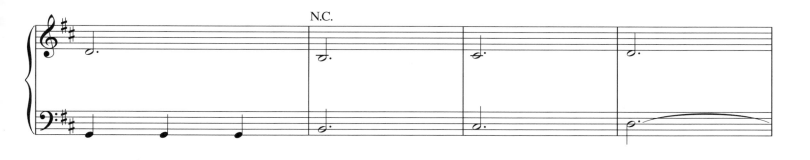

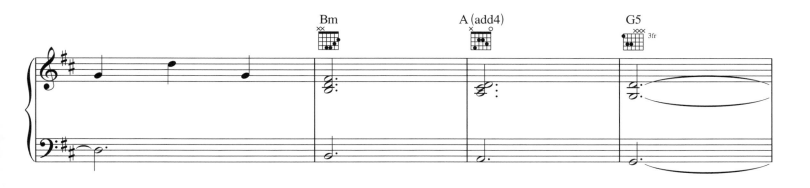

And I _____ don't want the world _____ to see _____ me

IS THIS LOVE

Words and Music by DAVID COVERDALE
and JOHN SYKES

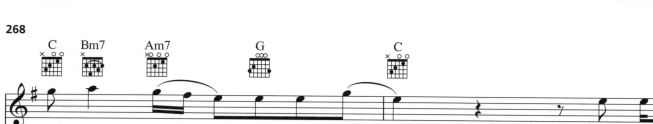

search-ing for? _____ Is this love _____ or am I

dream-ing? ___ This must be love, ___ 'cause it's real-ly got a hold on me, ___

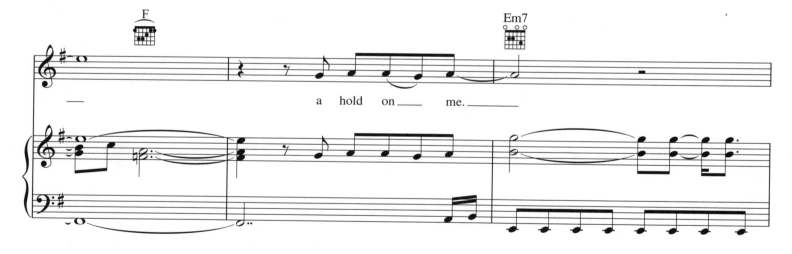

___ a hold on ___ me. _____

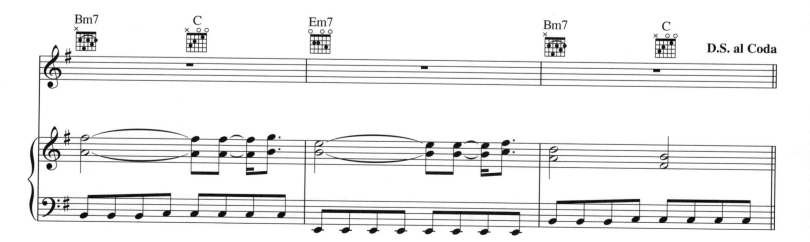

D.S. al Coda

ISLANDS IN THE STREAM

Words and Music by BARRY GIBB,
MAURICE GIBB and ROBIN GIBB

Baby, when I met you, there was peace un-known.___ I set out to get you with a

I can't live with-out you if the love has gone.___ Ev-'ry-thing is noth-ing when you

fine-tooth comb. I was soft in-side;___ there___ was some-thing go-ing on.___

got no one, and you walk in the night,___ slow-ly los-ing sight of the

IT MUST HAVE BEEN LOVE

Words and Music by
PER GESSLE

It must have been love, _____ but it's o - ver now. _____ Lay a whis-

KEEP ON LOVING YOU

Words and Music by
KEVIN CRONIN

LET'S GET IT ON

Words and Music by MARVIN GAYE
and ED TOWNSEND

Slow Soul beat

I've been real-ly try - in', ba - by, try-in' to hold _ back this feel-

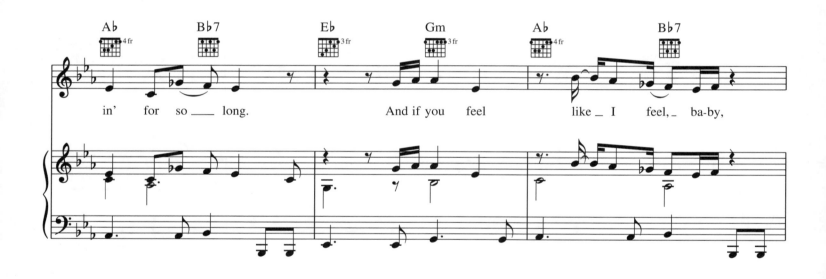

in' for so ___ long. And if you feel like _ I feel, _ ba-by,

then come on, _ on, _ come on. Ooh, _ let's get it on. Ow, ___

LOVE TO LOVE YOU, BABY

Words and Music by DONNA SUMMER,
GIORGIO MORODER and PETER BELLOTTE

LET'S STAY TOGETHER

Words and Music by AL GREEN,
WILLIE MITCHELL and AL JACKSON, JR.

LOVE BITES

Words and Music by STEVE CLARK,
PHIL COLLEN, JOE ELLIOTT,
R.J. LANGE and RICK SAVAGE

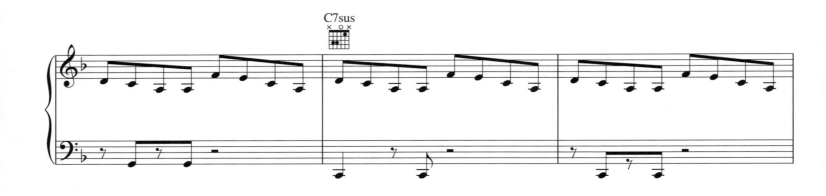

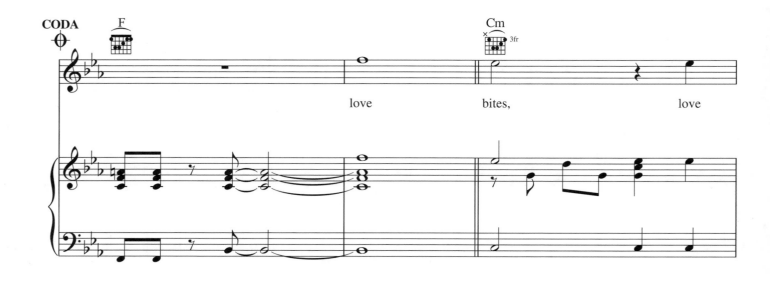

Repeat and Fade

Optional Ending

LOVE ME TENDER

Words and Music by ELVIS PRESLEY
and VERA MATSON

Love me ten - der, love me sweet,
Love me ten - der, love me long,
Love me ten - der, love me dear,
When at last my dreams come true,

nev - er let me go. You have made my
take me to your heart, for it's made there my
tell me you are mine. I'll be yours through
dar - ling, this I know: Hap - pi - ness will

LOVE WILL KEEP US TOGETHER

Words and Music by NEIL SEDAKA
and HOWARD GREENFIELD

Moderately

Love, / You, / will — love will keep us to-geth-er; / you be - long to me now; / be there to share for-ev - er;

think of me, babe, when-ev - er / ain't gon-na set you free now. / love will keep us to-geth-er. — some sweet-talk-in' guy comes a - long, / When those guys start hang-in' a-round, / Said it be-fore and I'll say it a-gain, while

sing-in' his song. / talk-in' me down, / oth-ers pre-tend, — Don't mess a - round; you got-ta be strong. / hear with your heart and you won't hear a sound. Just / I need you now and I'll need you then.

MANDY

Words and Music by SCOTT ENGLISH
and RICHARD KERR

MAYBE I'M AMAZED

Words and Music by
PAUL McCARTNEY

318

MORE THAN A FEELING

Words and Music by
TOM SCHOLZ

Medium Rock

I woke up this morn - ing and the sun was gone.____ I
So man - y peo - ple have come and gone;____ the

turned up the mu - sic to start my____ day.____ I
fac - es fade____ as to the years go____ by,____ yet

When I'm tired___ and think - ing cold, I hide in my mu - sic, for -

MORE THAN WORDS

Words and Music by NUNO BETTENCOURT
and GARY CHERONE

Original key: F# major. This edition has been transposed up one half-step to be more playable.

MY HEART WILL GO ON
(Love Theme from 'Titanic')
from the Paramount and Twentieth Century Fox Motion Picture TITANIC

Music by JAMES HORNER
Lyric by WILL JENNINGS

NEVER TEAR US APART

Words and Music by ANDREW FARRIS
and MICHAEL HUTCHENCE

NOBODY WANTS TO BE LONELY

Words and Music by DESMOND CHILD,
VICTORIA SHAW and GARY BURR

Male: Why? _____

Why? _____

Why? _____

Original key: Bb minor. This edition has been transposed down one half-step to be more playable.

OPEN ARMS

Words and Music by STEVE PERRY
and JONATHAN CAIN

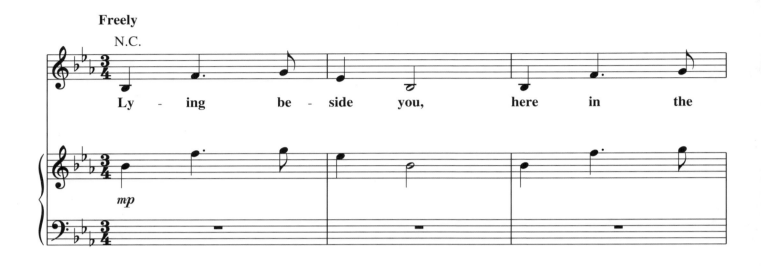

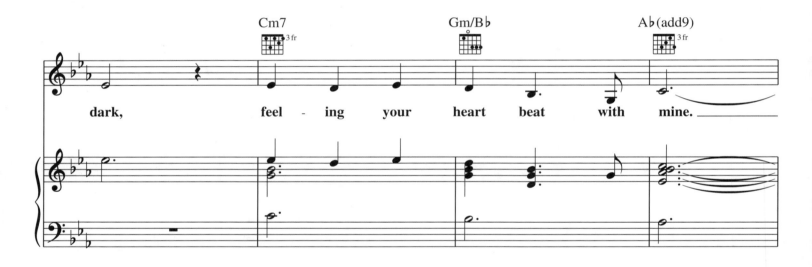

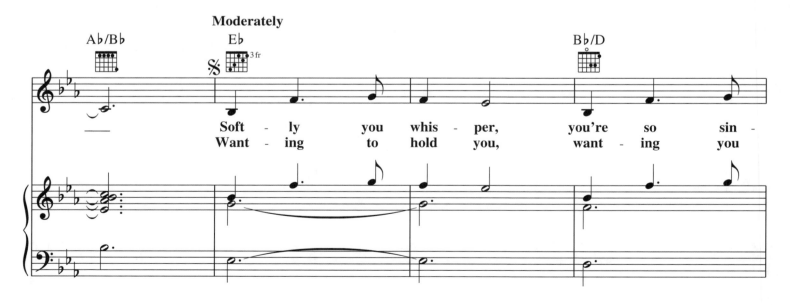

SHE'S GOT A WAY

Words and Music by
BILLY JOEL

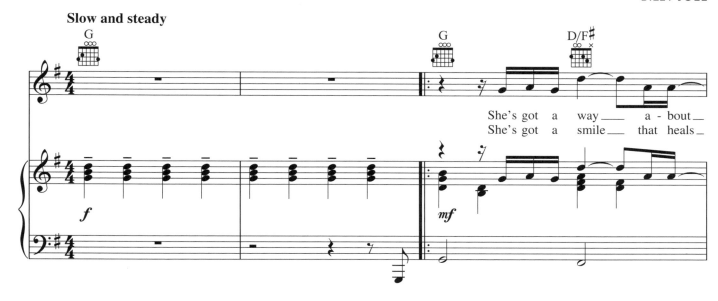

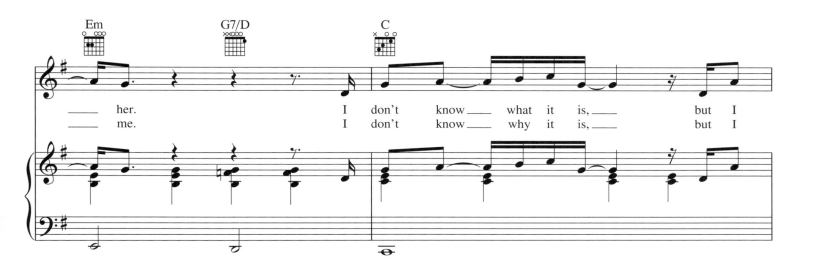

SAVE THE BEST FOR LAST

Words and Music by PHIL GALDSTON,
JON LIND and WENDY WALDMAN

SUPERSTAR

Words and Music by LEON RUSSELL
and BONNIE SHERIDAN

Long a - go _____ and oh _____ so _____ far a - way, _____
Lone - li - ness _____ is such a _____ sad af - fair, _____

I fell _____ in _____ love with you _____ be - fore the
and I _____ can hard - ly wait _____ to be with

SWEET CHILD O' MINE

Words and Music by W. AXL ROSE, SLASH, IZZY STRADLIN',
DUFF McKAGAN and STEVEN ADLER

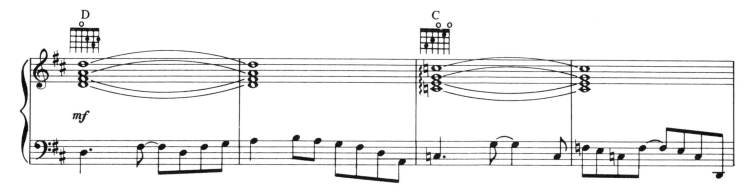

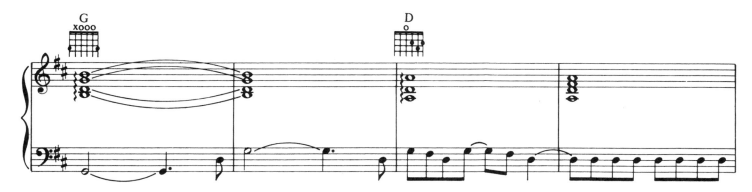

*Recorded a half step lower.

1. She's got a smile that it seems to me reminds me of child-hood
2. *See additional lyrics*

mem - o - ries, where ev - 'ry - thing was as fresh

Chorus

Whoa, whoa, whoa, sweet child o' mine.

Whoa, oh, oh, oh, sweet love o' mine.

To Coda

D.S. al Coda

Additional Lyrics

2. She's got eyes of the bluest skies, as if they thought of rain.
   I hate to look into those eyes and see an ounce of pain.
   Her hair reminds me of a warm safe place where as a child I'd hide,
   And pray for the thunder and the rain to quietly pass me by. *(To Chorus)*

THANK YOU

Words and Music by PAUL HERMAN
and DIDO ARMSTRONG

*Vocal written one octave higher than sung.

Original key: G# minor. This edition has been transposed up one half-step to be more playable.

Push the door; _ I'm home _ at _ last, _ and I'm soak - ing through _ and through. _

THAT'S THE WAY LOVE GOES

Words and Music by JAMES HARRIS III, TERRY LEWIS, JANET JACKSON,
JAMES BROWN, FRED WESLEY, CHARLES BOBBIT and JOHN STARKS

THIS I PROMISE YOU

Words and Music by
RICHARD MARX

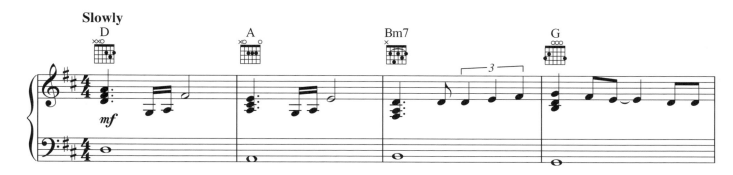

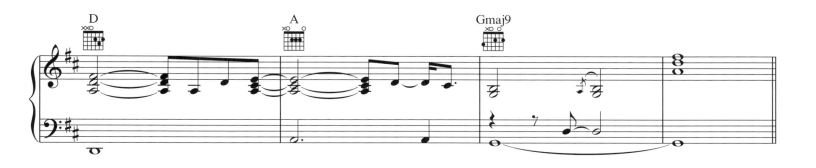

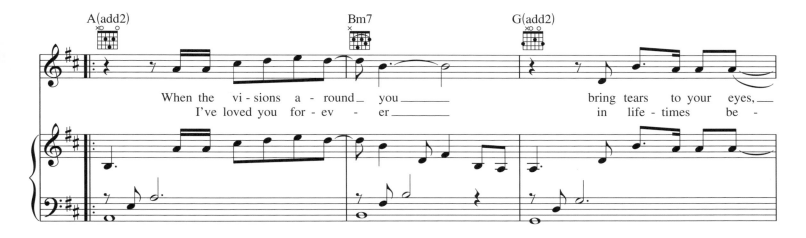

When the vi-sions a-round you bring tears to your eyes,
I've loved you for-ev - er in life-times be -

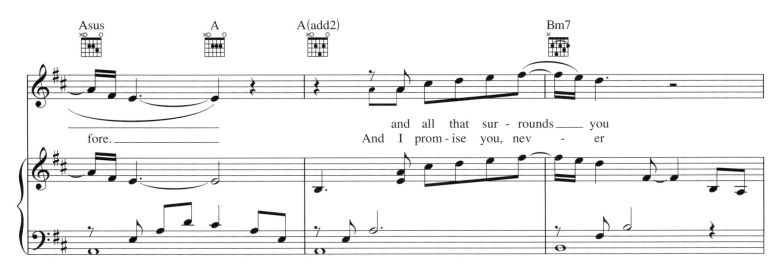

fore.
And I prom-ise you, nev - er

and all that sur-rounds you

G(add2)   Asus   A   Em7

are se-crets and lies,___   I'll be your strength,___   I
will you hurt an-y - more.___   give you my word.___

A7   D   A/C#   Bm7

I'll give you hope,___   keep-ing your faith___ when it's   gone._____   The
give you my heart.___   This is a bat - tle we've   won._____

1st time only

Em7   Gm6   Asus

one you should call___   was stand-ing here all___ a - long._____
And with this vow,___   for - ev - er has now___ be - gun. __

Asus   A   *§* D   A

___   And I will take___ you in my arms___ and
___   Just close your eyes___ each lov - ing day___ and

Instrumental

THINK OF LAURA

Words and Music by
CHRISTOPHER CROSS

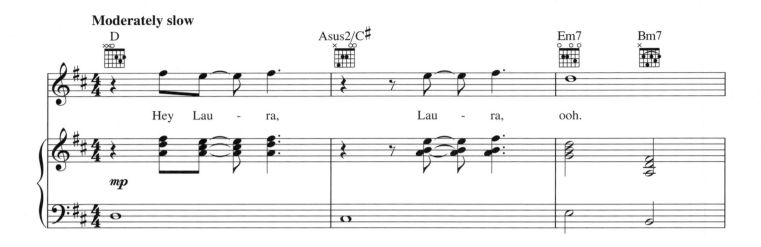

Hey Lau - ra, Lau - ra, ooh.

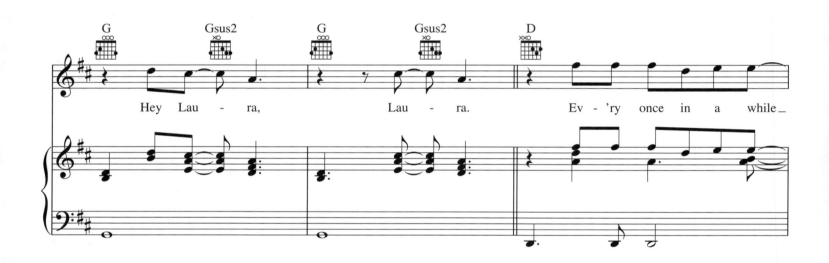

Hey Lau - ra, Lau - ra. Ev - 'ry once in a while___

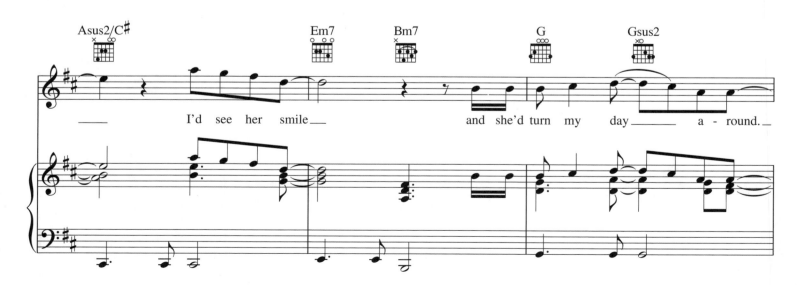

___ I'd see her smile___ and she'd turn my day_____ a - round.___

THREE TIMES A LADY

Words and Music by
LIONEL RICHIE

Slowly

Thanks for the

times that you've giv - en me. _____ The

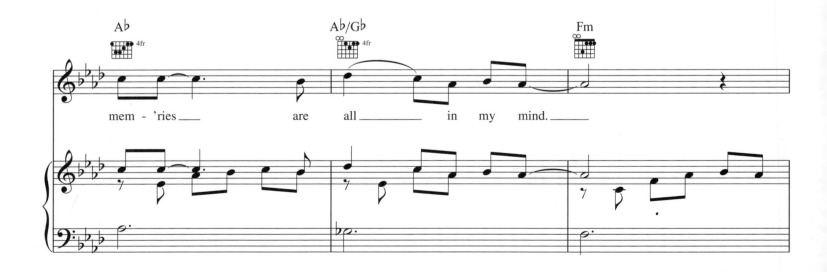

mem - 'ries _____ are all _____ in my mind. _____

TIME AFTER TIME

Words and Music by CYNDI LAUPER
and ROB HYMAN

(I've Had)
THE TIME OF MY LIFE
from DIRTY DANCING

Words and Music by FRANKE PREVITE,
JOHN DeNICOLA and DONALD MARKOWITZ

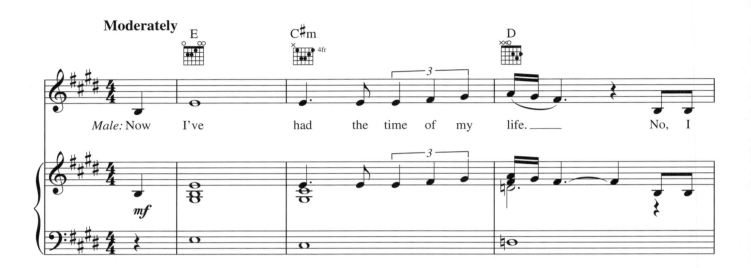

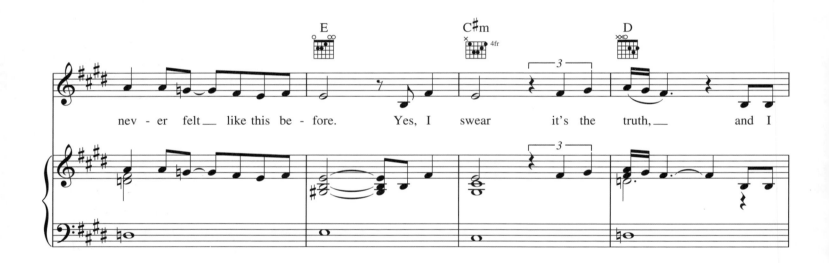

sy. _____

Both: Now with

pas - sion in our eyes _____ there's no way we could_ dis - guise _____ it se - cret -

ly. _____

So we

take each oth - er's hand _____ 'cause we seem to un - der - stand_ the ur - gen -

TO BE WITH YOU

Words and Music by ERIC MARTIN
and DAVID GRAHAME

TOTAL ECLIPSE OF THE HEART

Words and Music by
JIM STEINMAN

Turn a - round _____ Eve - ry now and then I get a
Turn a - round _____ Eve - ry now and then I get a
- part) *(Instrumental/Verse 3)*

lit - tle bit lone - ly and you're ne - ver com - ing round _____
lit - tle bit rest - less and I dream of some - thing wild _____

Turn a - round _____ Eve - ry now and then I get a
Turn a - round _____ Eve - ry now and then I get a

Verse 3:

Turn around
Every now and then I know you'll never be the boy you
always wanted to be
Turn around.
But every now and then I know you'll always be the only boy
who wanted me the way that I am
Turn around.
Every now and then I know there's no-one in the universe as
magical and wonderous as you
Turn around.
Every now and then I know there's nothing any better there's
nothing that I just wouldn't do

Chorus:

Turn around bright eyes
Every now and then I fall apart
Turn around bright eyes
Every now and then I fall apart

Middle:

And I need you now tonight, and I need you more than ever
And if you'll only hold me tight we'll be holding on forever
And we'll only be making it right cause we'll never be
wrong together
We can take it to the end of the line.
Your love is like a shadow on me all the time
I don't know what to do and I'm always in the dark
We're living in a powder keg and giving off sparks

I really need you tonight, forever's gonna start tonight,
forever's gonna start tonight

Once upon a time I was falling in love, but now I'm only
falling apart
Nothing I can do, a total eclipse of the heart
Once upon a time there was light in my life, but now
there's only love in the dark
Nothing I can say, a total eclipse of the heart
A total eclipse of the heart

Turn around bright eyes
Turn around bright eyes
Turn around.

UN-BREAK MY HEART

Words and Music by
DIANE WARREN

Don't leave me in ___ all this pain. ___ Don't leave me out ___ in the rain. ___
Take back that sad ___ word, "good - bye." ___ Bring back the joy ___ to my life. ___

UNCHAINED MELODY

from the Motion Picture UNCHAINED

Lyric by HY ZARET
Music by ALEX NORTH

Tempo I

WOMAN

Words and Music by
JOHN LENNON

Woman, I can hard-ly ex-press my mixed e-mo-tions at my
Woman, I know you un-der-stand the lit-tle child in-

thought-less-ness. Af-ter all, __ I'm for-ev-er in your debt. __ And
side the man. Please re-mem-ber, my life is in your hands. __ And

wom-an, I will try to ex-press __ my in-ner feel-ings and
wom-an, hold me close to your heart. __ How-ev-er dis-tant, don't

UNFORGETTABLE

Words and Music by
IRVING GORDON

WE BELONG

Words and Music by DAVID ERIC LOWDEN
and DANIEL NAVARRO

Moderately

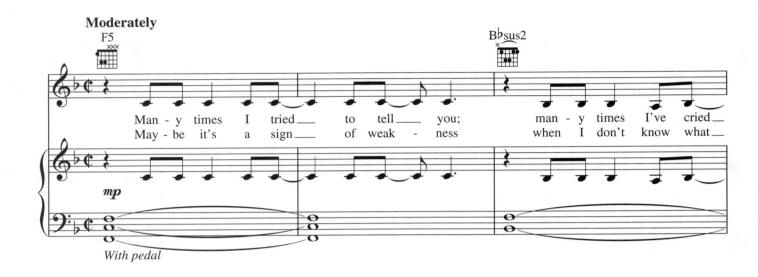

Man-y times I tried to tell you; man-y times I've cried
May-be it's a sign of weak-ness when I don't know what

a - lone. Al - ways I'm sur - prised how well you
to say. May - be I just would - n't know what to

cut my feel-ings to the bone. Don't wan - na leave
do with my strength an - y - way. Have we be - come

Close your eyes and try ___ to sleep ___ now.

Close your eyes and try ___ to dream. ___ Clear your mind and do ___

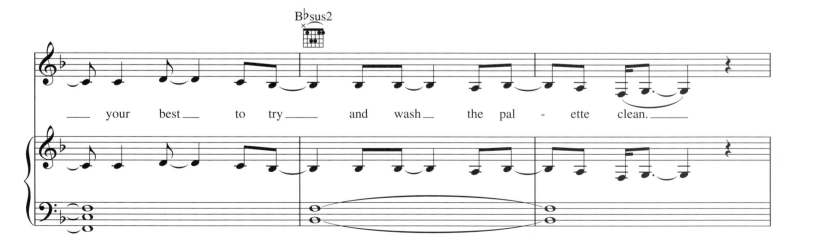

___ your best ___ to try ___ and wash ___ the pal - ette clean. ___

WONDERFUL TONIGHT

Words and Music by
ERIC CLAPTON

YOU ARE SO BEAUTIFUL

Words and Music by BILLY PRESTON
and BRUCE FISHER

YOU ARE THE SUNSHINE OF MY LIFE

Words and Music by
STEVIE WONDER

YOU DON'T BRING ME FLOWERS

Words by NEIL DIAMOND,
MARILYN BERGMAN and ALAN BERGMAN
Music by NEIL DIAMOND

Slowly and freely

YOU'RE IN MY HEART

Words and Music by
ROD STEWART

I did-n't know what day it was when you walked
I took all those hab-its of yours that in the be-

YOU'RE STILL THE ONE

Words and Music by SHANIA TWAIN
and R.J. LANGE

YOU'RE THE FIRST, THE LAST, MY EVERYTHING

Words and Music by P. STERLING RADCLIFFE,
TONY SEPE and BARRY WHITE

2nd Chorus:

In you I find so many things,
A love so new only you could bring.
Can't you see if you . . . you make me feel this way,
You're like a fresh morning dew
Or a brand new day.

I see so many ways that I
Can love you till the day I die.
You're my reality,
Yet I'm lost in a dream.
You're The First, The Last, My Everything.

YOUR SONG

Words and Music by ELTON JOHN
and BERNIE TAUPIN

Slow, but with a beat

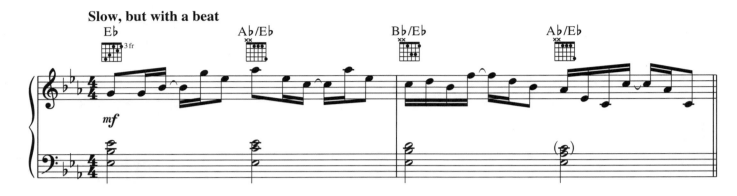

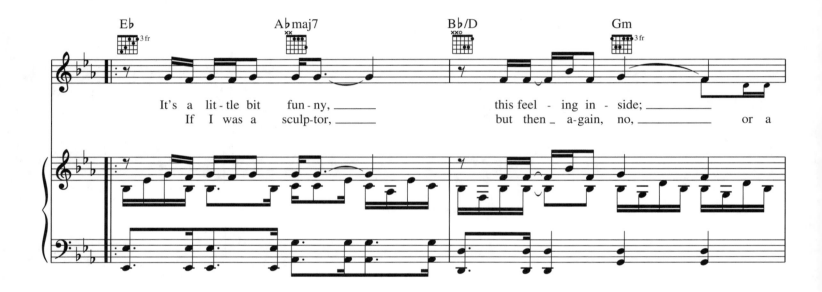

It's a lit-tle bit fun-ny, _____ this feel - ing in - side; _____
If I was a sculp-tor, _____ but then _ a-gain, no, _____ or a

I'm not one of those _ who _ can eas-i-ly hide. _____
man who makes po - tions in a trav-el - in' show, _____ I

YOU'RE THE ONE THAT I WANT

from GREASE

Words and Music by
JOHN FARRAR

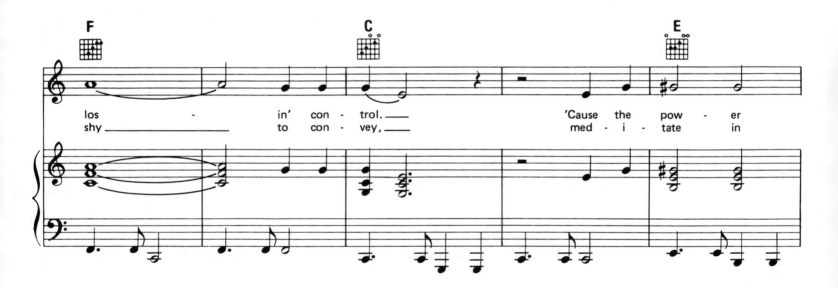

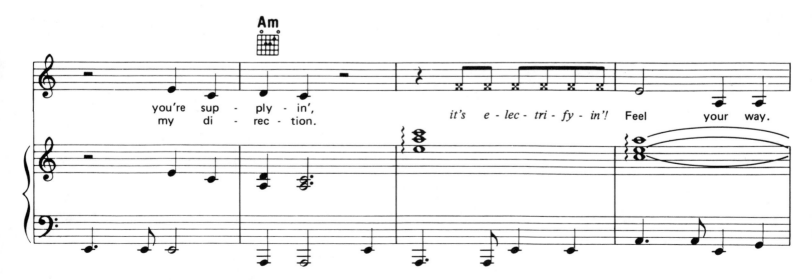